Original title:
The Snowbound Heart

Copyright © 2024 Creative Arts Management OÜ
All rights reserved.

Author: Charles Whitfield
ISBN HARDBACK: 978-9916-94-528-5
ISBN PAPERBACK: 978-9916-94-529-2

## Charmed by the Chill

Snowflakes tumble like a clown,
Covering the sleepy town.
My coffee's cold, can you believe?
I laugh while I grind and sieve.

Mittens mismatched, what a sight,
Dancing penguins in the night.
Hot cocoa spills, a foamy wave,
Oh, winter, you misbehave!

Icicles hang like crystal swords,
Frosty breath revokes the hoards.
Snowmen wobble, faces drawn,
Who knew winter was so fawn?

Sledding down the haunted hill,
Each bump brings the loudest shrill.
With every fall, my cheeks get red,
Giggles echo in my head!

## A Haiku for the Frostbound

Winter's chill arrives,
Snowmen dance with delight,
Wipe that grin from face!

**Imprints on the Icy Path**

Feet like clumsy elves,
Slipping, sliding in style,
Yelling, 'Look at me!'
Fallen frozen joy!

**Snow-Laden Sentiments**

Snowflakes land with sass,
Whispering snowy jokes,
Chill can't hold us back,
Laughter fills the air!

## **Heart Closets in the Cold**

Winter coats on rack,
Hiding hearts so frosty,
But beneath the layers,
Hearts bloom, oh so bold!

## **Hibernating Emotions**

In a cozy nook, emotions snore,
They wrapped themselves up, can't take much more.
Snowflakes dance, yet they yawn and sleep,
While popcorn kernels start to creep.

The heart's in a blanket, so fluffy and wide,
It plays hide and seek with the pride inside.
Laughter echoes, but muffled is fun,
As it hibernates under the frosty sun.

## **Veils of Winter's Breathe**

Winter's breath fogs the mind's eye,
While hearts wear layers, oh my, oh my!
With puffy coats and hats so round,
Emotions wander, lost and found.

Sledding downhill with glee and a glide,
But in truth, the heart just wants to hide.
Snowman grins, but he's not so bright,
While our hearts frolic in a snowy fright.

## **Glacial Lullabies**

The ice sings softly as jingles appear,
While love does the cha-cha with frozen cheer.
Chill it may, but spirits are bold,
As they trip on the frost, over all things cold.

Snowflakes boogie, round and bright,
While hearts chime in, "Hey, that looks right!"
In this frosty dance, we take our stance,
Even if our feet get lost in the prance.

## Heartstrings in the Cold

When frostbite nips at the heartstrings taut,
They shiver and shake—what was that thought?
A penguin slips on ice with a flair,
While our love does cartwheels—if it can dare.

With scarves that tangle in giggles and glows,
A snowball fight breaks out in the throes.
Hearts tease the frost, playfully bold,
Chasing warmth in this winter of cold.

## **Icicles Hanging from Memory**

Icicles dangle like old tales,
Telling stories of winter gales.
Falling off roofs with a comical grace,
Reminding us of life's silly race.

Snowflakes twirl in a dance so absurd,
Pretending to be the most graceful bird.
They land on my nose, how delightfully weird,
Nature's own jokes, I can't help but jeered.

## **Hope Within the Flurry**

Amid the flurries, I spot a flair,
A snowman grinning, without a care.
His carrot nose leans askew,
In a snowball fight, he's surely due!

Chasing my dog, bounding about,
He thinks every snowflake is a shout!
With each wild leap and icy glide,
We both lose balance and tumble with pride!

## In the Stillness of Snow

In the stillness, there's laughter in air,
Beneath white blankets, I stumble and stare.
An avalanche of laundry takes the stage,
With socks as my cast, oh what a rage!

I build a fortress, a bit lopsided,
With cupids inside that are quite misguided.
Maybe they'll guard me from a slip,
Or just throw snowballs during their trip.

### **Melodies in White Silence**


Quiet as kittens, the snow falls down,
Blanketing the chaos all over town.
A snow angel flops, a child's delight,
With arms wide open, ready for flight.

Frozen giggles echo in frosty air,
As snowballs fly without a care.
The winters may chill, but spirits soar,
In this winter wonderland, who could ask for more?

**Frozen Whispers**

In the chilly air, I hear you giggle,
Snowflakes dance and make us wiggle.
A snowman's nose, not quite a carrot,
Too many laughs, we start to parrot.

Mittens lost, oh what a plight!
We chase them down with pure delight.
Icicles hang like silly pens,
Writing tales of snowball friends.

## Winter's Embrace

Wrapped up tight in scarves and hats,
We play with snow, like fluffy cats.
Hot cocoa spills, we laugh and squeal,
Our winter bonding is a big deal.

Frosted noses, rosy cheeks,
We chat about the weather leaks.
Penguins slide, trying to soar,
While we build forts to even the score.

## Chilled Echoes of Love

Your hat flies off, the wind's a tease,
We chase it down with giggles and wheeze.
Love notes scribbled on icy glass,
How do they say, "Please let this pass?"

Snowflakes land, a dance in flight,
We giggle in the pallid light.
Two frozen hearts, we shiver bright,
With snowball fights that ignite the night.

**Frosted Memories**

Skipping on ice with little fear,
Each tumble brings a laugh, a cheer.
Sledding down on a lunch tray spree,
We glide like pros, or so we decree!

Memories freeze but hearts stay warm,
Through winter's chill, there's always charm.
With laughter ringing, let's not forget,
These frosted times we won't regret.

## Love's Lantern in the Winter

I saw you slip on ice and glide,
You twirled like a dancer, oh what a ride!
With snowflakes falling and cheeks so red,
You laughed so hard, forgot what you said.

The hot cocoa spilled, a chocolate mess,
You grinned so wide, I must confess.
With laughter echoing in frosty air,
We built a snowman with style and flair.

Your mittens matched, a bright surprise,
We painted the town with snowball fights.
Each playful throw, we both did squeal,
As we fell in love, that's how it feels.

From frozen toes to warm hearts' glow,
In winter's grasp, our fondness did grow.
So here's our love in this chill and frolic,
With lanterns of laughter, quite iconic!

## Serene Stillness of the Heart

Your hat was fuzzy, mine too tight,
We laughed and stumbled in pure delight.
In silence, the snowflakes began to play,
Turning our cheeks to rosy array.

We watched the bunnies hop in fright,
As we slipped and slid into a snowball fight.
Covered in white, we giggled and rolled,
A comedy of warmth in the winter's cold.

With every flake, a joke unspooled,
As we sipped tea, feeling quite the fool.
In serene stillness, love found its track,
With hearts so light, we never looked back.

So here we sit in this frosty nook,
Sharing our laughter like a storybook.
Joy wrapped us tight in the coldest of nights,
Our hearts transform with these playful flights.

## **Glimmers of Light in Frozen Nights**

The moon peeked out, the stars all laughed,
As we both wandered, each step a craft.
With twinkling lights strung on snowy trees,
We danced like cornflakes blown by the breeze.

Your breath made clouds, I found it cute,
We played hide and seek in our warmest boots.
Glimmers of joy in the cold night air,
As frostbite nipped with a cheeky flair.

Hot cider sipped, but yours was spiked,
You winked, and in that moment, I hiked.
With giggles echoing in this winter delight,
We stumbled back home, hearts full and light.

So here we bask in the frosty glow,
Glimmers of laughter in the swirling snow.
In this chilly embrace, adventures ignite,
Two goofy souls in frozen delight.

## The Silent Dance of Chilled Souls

As winter wrapped the world in white,
We cranked up tunes, danced through the night.
With each twirl, I stepped on your toes,
And laughed so hard, that anything goes.

Your scarf unraveled like spaghetti strands,
Snowflakes caught in our outstretched hands.
We spun in place, a slapstick ballet,
With winter beneath us, we found our way.

The cold air nipped, but our spirits soared,
With silent dances, love's song explored.
We tumbled and rolled, no need for grace,
Side-splitting joy, etched on each face.

So when the chill wrapped us like a scroll,
In frosty silence, we danced as a whole.
Two chilled souls in laughter, not a worry in sight,
In this ridiculous play, we took flight.

## **Love Letters in the Snow**

I wrote you a note, it got lost in the flake,
A heart made of ice, for my silly mistake.
I sealed it with giggles, forgot it was bright,
It drifted away, like a kite in the night.

Your laughter lays thick, like a blanket of white,
You tripped on my words, what a comical sight.
With mittens on hands, we'd scribble and play,
Our love gets more silly, come frost or come spray.

# Reawakening in the Thaw

As spring starts to tease, winter's giggle retreats,
The snowmen are melting, revealing their feats.
A lost mitten found, hidden deep in the ice,
To warm up our hands, oh, isn't that nice?

With puddles like mirrors, we splash and we cheer,
Each drip is a story, each laugh near a tear.
The thaw brings a chuckle, as winter turns shy,
Our snowbound existence, now dances on high.

## Snowbound Soliloquies

In the silence of snow, I ponder my fate,
A snowball of thoughts, just don't make me wait.
The squirrels throw shade, from their frosty high perch,
While I yell at the sky, does it come with a search?

I talk to the trees, they just laugh at my plea,
What's cold for a heart, feels like warm, silly tea.
So here I will sit, on this cushy white throne,
Making snow angels, all covered in foam.

## **Chilling Echoes of the Past**

Old footprints behind, like a comic parade,
Each step tells a joke, lingering and delayed.
The snowflakes they tease, swirling laughs in the air,
With each icy whisper, I'm caught in a dare.

I slip on a patch, oh what a grand view,
Down I go tumbling, as if I just grew.
Yet laughter is warm, as we scoff at the chill,
In the frosty embrace, we're just odd, yet still.

## **Heartbeats Beneath the Ice**

In winter's grip, my heart does dance,
A leap, a skip, a frosty prance.
I trip on snow, my face meets ground,
The slush and giggles all around.

With every chill, I feel so bold,
But slipping on ice, I'm far from gold.
My love is warm, but oh, so sly,
She laughs and calls me 'Frosty Guy!'

I build a snowman, tall and grand,
But he's got a hat that's made of sand.
He tips and topples, oh what a sight,
We argue who's the wittiest tonight.

So here's to hearts that skip and slide,
In winter's wonder, with laughs as our guide.
Amidst the snow, our love shines bright,
With every slip, we feel delight.

## A Silence Wrapped in White

The world is still, all wrapped in fluff,
But in my heart, there's just enough.
Silly snowflakes fall and tease,
A snowball fight, oh what a breeze!

My dog darts in, a furry blur,
He leaps and rolls with quite a stir.
While I'm all geared up in layers tight,
He zips around, such pure delight!

We toss the snow, like small white bombs,
It's time for giggles, there are no qualms.
With frosty cheeks and rosy noses,
Even the snow-woman's giggle dozes.

Yet in this hush, we share a glance,
With hearts that giggle, we start to dance.
For in this silence, we're far from grim,
Our laughter echoes, a winter hymn.

## Beneath the Winter Sky

Underneath the stars all bright,
I wear my scarf and hold on tight.
But as I trip, I hide my fall,
The snowflakes whisper, 'Don't tell at all!'

Hot cocoa's steam, a sweet embrace,
Yet I spill it all, what a disgrace!
My s'mores are charred, they toast too long,
I laugh it off; what could go wrong?

Through branches bare, I dash and spin,
While chubby cheeks greet winter's win.
Snow angels made with flapping arms,
We giggle at all of winter's charms.

With every breath, we share our cheer,
Each frosted laugh brings us all near.
For when winter throws its icy jive,
Our funny hearts are very much alive!

## **Dreams in the Snowdrifts**

In dreams, I slip on icy floors,
And wake to see the snow once more.
A throne of snow, I sit up high,
But only birds can hear my sigh.

The flakes conspire, a cheeky crew,
To hide my hat, it's tried and true.
With every layer I put in place,
They fashion snowmen with a silly face.

As snowflakes swirl in playful puffs,
I'm left to deal with all the huffs.
My snowshoes squeak in protest loud,
While I chase dreams beyond the crowd.

Yet here I stand, a winter king,
My heart adorned with joy to bring.
Amidst the chill, we find our tune,
With every laugh beneath the moon.

## Echoes in the Silent Woods

In the woods where whispers roam,
A squirrel claims a twig for home.
He slips and lands in powdery fluff,
While birds chuckle, "That's quite enough!"

As snowflakes dance with a wiggly spree,
The trees giggle at the sight to see.
A rabbit hops by, looks quite bemused,
"I swear I wore this coat, I'm not confused!"

With frosty breath, the critters play,
Catching snowballs with a zany sway.
A hedgehog rolls, then gets up slow,
"Next time I'll stick to summer's glow!"

The sun peeks out, a warm surprise,
"Oh look! It's time for snowman ties!"
They band together, or so they say,
But end up wrapped in their snow-filled play!

## Soft Footsteps Through Snowfall

With boots that squeak, I stroll along,
The fluffy white sings its own song.
I tiptoe here and take a chance,
Oh look! A pie-shaped snowman dance!

A cat with earmuffs checks the scene,
Sipping cocoa, acting quite serene.
She winks at me as if to say,
"In this winter, I rule the fray!"

Snow angels lie like fashion faux pas,
Wings askew, like a fashion star.
While laughter echoes in the cold,
"Fashion's fun but check the mold!"

As I amuse the snow with tricks,
A friendly dog joins, feeling slick.
He jumps and rolls, a furry blizzard,
With wagging tails, we laugh with glee, absurd!

## Snowflakes and Secrets

Each flake that falls has a tale to tell,
They swirl and twirl, casting a spell.
A gossiping breeze sneaks in the night,
"What happens here? Oh what a sight!"

The snowman boasts of carrot jewels,
While children gather, much like fools.
One whispers, "Did you see that flip?"
Another laughs, "Now that's a trip!"

In the quiet, secrets do arise,
Under those blankets, surprise, surprise!
The snow conceals a world of fun,
'Til spring arrives and melts it done!

So here we sit, with snowball fights,
Cracking jokes and absurd delights.
With frosty air, we cheer and shout,
"Who needs a heart? Just laugh it out!"

## A Heart in Deep Freeze

In winter's grip, my heart feels tight,
It melts with laughter, warm and bright.
With icicles hanging like frozen tears,
I shake it off, dispelling fears.

The thermos spills a cocoa flood,
The snowmen chuckle, "What a dud!"
But laughter keeps the frost at bay,
Making winter whims a grand display.

A penguin slides with all his might,
While mocking geese take off in flight.
"Chill out!" I hear one proud goose cry,
As snowflakes tumble, oh my, oh my!

With mittens snug, we join the plot,
In this frozen world, we find a lot.
Heart warmed by giggles on this spree,
Who knew a chill could feel so free?

## **Storms of Recollection**

Flakes fall fast, a white confetti,
Dance around like toddlers, unsteady.
Memories swirl in a mighty storm,
Laughter echoes where hearts stay warm.

With each drift, my thoughts collide,
Of snowballs thrown and sleds that glide.
I trip and tumble, a sight so absurd,
Yet in the chaos, joy's never blurred.

The snowman smiles, a carrot-nosed clown,
As I'm buried deep, down I go down.
Frosty breath speaks of frozen dreams,
In icy castles, life's not as it seems.

But here I chuckle, in winter's embrace,
Each flake a memory, a giggling face.
Through storms of laughter, I wade with glee,
Snowbound moments, just snowing me free.

# Heartbeats Under Blanket Snow

Under the blankets, a fortress of fluff,
Heartbeats echo, cozy and tough.
Outside it howls, but we hum along,
Inside we giggle with our favorite song.

The dog's buried deep, in layers of fur,
He snores like a beast, with not a single purr.
A snowball fight? Oh, what a plan!
But first, let's nap, because we can!

In the fluff of our fortress, warmth is supreme,
Slippers abound, it's the ultimate dream.
As flakes twirl wildly around our abode,
We find our own rhythm, our own little road.

With mugs of cocoa, we huddle real tight,
Counting each snowflake that falls with delight.
The world's a blizzard, but here we giggle,
In our cozy kingdom, where hearts dance and wiggle.

## In the Cold, a Glimpse of Warmth

Icicles hang like lollipops bright,
As I stumble past, a comical sight.
My mittens mismatched, my scarf a hot mess,
Yet in all this madness, I am blessed.

Snow boots squish, with each clumsy step,
I flap like a penguin, I'm no adept.
But oh, what a thrill, with giggles that fly,
As I launch a snowball, aimed at the sky!

Birds in their jackets, all fluff and chime,
Watch me flail, I'm a joke every time.
Yet around me, warmth in chuckles takes root,
When laughter erupts and my face looks like fruit!

In the chilly air, we share one big grin,
Hearts made of snowflakes, bundled within.
There's joy in this frosty, humorous tale,
For amidst all the ice, love will prevail.

## **Remembering Beneath the Drifts**

Beneath the drifts, a memory stirs,
A time we laughed till our sides were in blurs.
Snowball battles turned into sledding spree,
Who'd guess that winter's such fun to see?

Frosted windows hold secrets of glee,
Voices of friendship, as warm as can be.
We'd race down slopes, with a whoop and a cheer,
Each tumble and flip only sharpened our cheer.

Laughter escapes like the chill in the air,
Mixing our joys with snowflakes to share.
Memories parked on the snowy white beds,
Making snow angels, dreaming with heads.

So here's to the drifts where our hearts intertwine,
In the midst of the cold, where our giggles align.
Though snowflakes may melt, our laughs never cease,
In the warmth of the winter, we find our release.

## In the Silence, a Flame Glows

In a frosty nook, we sit,
With cocoa cups, and laughter split,
The marshmallows float like happy boats,
In our cozy world, that's full of quotes.

Outside the snowflakes tumble and swirl,
They dance like squirrels in a snowy whirl,
My fingers cold, I grab your scarf,
You claim it's mine, let's hear the laugh!

The fire crackles, wood pops and hisses,
Your nose turns red, it almost misses,
Trying to sip with a frosty grin,
You spill the hot drink, what a win!

We whisper secrets, chuckle and joke,
In this winter chill, hearts stoke,
A perfect night, just you and me,
Snowbound? Nah, we're wild and free!

## **Bound Together in Winter's Grip**

Two bundled up like sausages tight,
With fluff all around, we can't ignite,
Our laughter echoes in the blustery breeze,
While snowballs fly, like sneezes with ease.

We waddle through drifts, like ducks in a row,
You slip on the ice, oh no, don't go!
But laughter erupts, you bounce right back,
This winter dance, we're a hilariously whack.

Hot chocolate spills, we wear it like art,
A fashion statement, that's how we start,
With marshmallows clinging, like dreams on our coats,
In this icy realm, we're two silly goats.

A snowman awaits with a carrot for a nose,
We give him a scarf, he strikes a pose,
With mittens all mismatched, he can't complain,
In winter's grip, it's a chuckle, a gain!

## Echoing through the Winter Woods

In the silent woods, where snowflakes dwell,
We try to yell, but it's a soft spell,
Echoes of giggles bounce off the trees,
As we trip over roots, and tumble with ease.

The snowman's so tall, he needs a hat,
But there's a raccoon, might chase us, imagine that!
We build him a snow pal, with a grin so wide,
Our frosty creation, perfect snowy pride.

With each frosty breath, comes a cloud that puffs,
Your face gets puffy, I call your bluff,
You claim it's the cold, I see it as fun,
In this winter wonder, we laugh 'til it's done.

A snowball fight, oh, here comes a blast,
But you missed the target, what a cast!
In these winter woods, our joy can't be bound,
With echoes of laughter, warmth does abound.

## **Ribbons of Snowy Light**

Ribbons of snow swirl in the air,
Twirling and twinkling, without a care,
We chase the flakes, like kids on a spree,
As if they're whispers that play hide and seek.

Your hat's on sideways, it's lost its flair,
I giggle so hard, it's hard to bear,
With boots that squish, we stomp the ground,
In our winter wonder, joy is profound.

The icicles hang like nature's bling,
While we dance in circles, and laugh, and sing,
You slip on the ice, it's a glorious sight,
But your laughter's the best, keeps me feeling light.

So here's to winter, with all its bliss,
Snowflakes and giggles, you can't miss,
In ribbons of light, our hearts all play,
In this frosted land, we merrily stay!

## **Portraits Painted in White**

Frosty faces wave hello,
Puffy cheeks all aglow,
Snowmen strut with carrot snouts,
Doing dance with silly clouts.

Fluffy flakes fall from the sky,
Covering the world up high,
Snowball fights with gleeful cheer,
Watch out for that sneaky sphere!

Two kids slip on icy ground,
Laughter echoes all around,
A plump pup joins in the fun,
Skidding 'til the day is done.

Winter's canvas, bright and bold,
Painted tales that never get old,
With each flake, a story starts,
Crafted from our snowy hearts.

## **Constellations of Frozen Stars**

Twinkling lights hang from the frost,
Each one sparkling, none are lost,
Look up high, see snowflakes whirl,
Creating art with every twirl.

Frozen laughs and chilly grins,
Riding sleds, we all win!
Yet a snowbank hides a prank,
As friends slip down with joyful clank.

Stars blink down, their laughter bright,
While we gear up for another fight,
Snowballs launched like shooting stars,
Ring around the frosty cars.

Hot cocoa waits in cozy nooks,
And snowflakes spin like children's books,
Who knew winter could bring such glee?
Under frosty skies, just you and me.

## **Dreams Encased in Ice**

In the chill, we make a wish,
For snowflakes dance and twirl with swish,
A castle built from frozen dreams,
Where laughter echoes, or so it seems.

Polar bears in scarves parade,
Waltzing through the chilly glade,
A frosty fox with mischief planned,
Slides down slopes, never to stand.

Chilly thoughts, we giggle tight,
Having fun till late at night,
The winter moon, a spotlight bright,
Illuminating snowy sights.

A snow-angel's giggle, pure and clear,
Caught in winter's cozy sphere,
Hairstyles formed with frozen dew,
Who needs summer? Not me or you!

## Snowbound Stories of Old

Gather 'round the crackling fire,
Sharing tales that never tire,
Of brave knights in fluffy armor,
Chasing foes that are just charmer.

Legend says the flurries dance,
When snowmen are given a chance,
To skate on ice with dreams so bright,
Spinning quietly through the night.

Cousins wrapped in scarves so tight,
Challenge each to snowy fight,
Laughter rings, the world's a stage,
Winter's warmth fills every page.

As snowflakes tumble, tales are spun,
Each laugh mapped in frosty fun,
With every flake, a joy we mold,
In stories of winter's grip, retold.

## Frosty Reveries

In the chill of winter's bite,
Snowflakes dance in pure delight.
There's a snowman with a grin,
Who wears my hat, oh what a sin!

Sledding down, I scream with glee,
A snowball fights a chance to be.
But slipping on the icy ground,
I tumble, laughter all around!

Hot cocoa warms my frosty toes,
While outside all the chaos grows.
The dog leaps high, a snowy beast,
Who claims my scarf—he's such a feast!

Friends all gather, making jokes,
We reminisce of youthful folks.
With every flake, a story clear,
In fun-filled snow, we shed a tear!

## **A Symphony of Snowdrifts**

The flakes descend like tiny jokes,
Building mountains of frosty pokes.
A symphony of giggles in the air,
While frozen fingers grasp with care.

Snowballs whiz, a flighty dance,
I throw one at a friend by chance.
They duck, but my aim is true,
Now they're a snowman, through and through!

Icicles dangle, sharp and spry,
A toothpick for the icecream pie.
But my tongue got stuck, oh what a plight!
A frozen lollipop—it's quite the sight!

We dance around the winter glow,
Each snow drift masking all our woe.
In playful chaos, we embrace the fun,
Each winter moment, like a joke, well done!

## Time Stopped in the Cold

Tick-tock, but not today,
For frozen clocks have lost their way.
While icicles hang like bags of gold,
I sip warm tea, a tale retold.

The cat leaps high, a crazy sprite,
Into the snow, oh what a sight!
As he wiggles, paws all soft,
I ponder how the world is oft.

In this winter wonder, time stands still,
We share our secrets, laughs to fill.
But when I stand, the ground gives way,
I'm corkscrewed back where I lay!

A blizzard of chuckles fills the room,
As friends arrive to cue the boom.
With every freeze, I lift the glass,
To toast the joy that will not pass!

## Reflections on a Snowy Pond

The surface perfectly reflects the scene,
Where snowflakes hint at wonders, pristine.
A pair of ducks in woolly fun,
Skate across, a fowlity run!

They quack and flip, in a comical show,
While giggling kids all lined up in a row.
I toss some bread, they swim with glee,
But they're fashion critics, what a spree!

With each waddle, they steal the show,
As laughter rings, our hearts aglow.
But slipping on the pond's edge, a fumble,
Into the snow—oh my, what a tumble!

We gather 'round the pond so bright,
Reflecting joy in the frosty light.
Our hearts warm up beneath the chill,
As snowflakes swirl, we laugh still!

## A Canvas of White Wishes

In the yard, snow piled high,
Snowmen with noses askew,
Children laughing, a gleeful cry,
Mittens lost, but spirits flew.

Sledding down the hill, what a sight,
Tumbling over, giggles burst,
Snowball fights until twilight,
Hot cocoa dreams, we quench our thirst.

Carrots for noses, who knew?
Frosty frowns that melt away,
The snowflakes dance, a lively crew,
Winter's gags in a playful sway.

Racing home, cheeks aglow,
Fingers numb, but hearts run free,
Snowy tales of friends in tow,
Frosty fun, a jubilee!

## Snowflakes and Silent Sweetness

Snowflakes falling, a soft surprise,
Drifting down like whispered dreams,
Just don't catch one in your eyes,
Or risk the start of frozen screams!

Hot chocolate spills - oh, what a sight,
Marshmallows swim, a sweet delight,
Slippery sidewalks, hold on tight,
Watch that last step - oops, goodnight!

Warming up by fireside glow,
Chasing cats with snowy hands,
What will the neighbors think? Oh no!
Sledding shenanigans, breakdance lands!

The snow's a canvas, we are the art,
From play to mess, we fill the air,
Blankets tossed and winter's heart,
In laughter, we find warmth to share.

## Resilient in the Frost

Bundled up in mismatched gear,
Laughter echoes through the chill,
A snowflake's touch, a hint of cheer,
Who'll brave the cold? We know we will!

Snow forts rise, defenses made,
Teamwork strife, who will prevail?
Snowball battles, plans are laid,
Victory tastes like winter's ale!

Breath like smoke, a dancing plume,
Yet inside, a hidden grin,
For all the fun, there's room for gloom,
Just watch out for that sly snowbin!

Race to the hill, against the clock,
A tumble, laughter fills the air,
Frosty kisses, beneath the rock,
We emerge, the winter's flair!

## **Buried Feelings**

Under snow, secrets lie deep,
Feelings frozen, awaiting the thaw,
But in this chill, we'll take a leap,
To toss a snowball, to hear the awe.

In the drifts, I find my heart,
Whirling 'round in starlit white,
Buried feelings, let's now restart,
In snow's soft grip, we take flight.

Snow angels spread their wings wide,
Imprints left in frosty glee,
Funny how laughter will abide,
With love engraved in snowballs, you see?

Marching home, our cheeks are red,
In winter's play, our hearts excite,
For buried feelings, no longer dread,
In snowy storms, we find delight!

## Hidden Hopes Beneath Frost

Under layers of fuzz and white,
A penguin's dream to take a flight.
Snowflakes dance, but he's a penguin,
Stuck in this chilly, frozen spin.

The squirrels wear coats, so dapper,
While rabbits laugh, what a caper!
Winter's chill brings funny sights,
As frosty critters share their lights.

Icicles hang like daggers sharp,
While snowmen play and grab their harp.
A winter's joke, oh what a tease,
They've lost their hats, oh, what a breeze!

Hot cocoa spills, a slippery slide,
Penguins waddle, full of pride.
With cocoa mustaches, they combine,
These hidden hopes of winter's shine.

## **A Tapestry of Winter Dreams**

In knitted hats and socks so warm,
Snowball battles take their form.
But one brave soul with shovels bright,
Just wants to sculpt a snowman right.

The snowflakes giggle as they fall,
While children slide and trip, a brawl.
A sideways glance leads to a face,
Of snow in shoes, what a disgrace!

Polar bears on frozen lakes,
Ice skating badly, oh what mistakes!
They tip and tumble, off they go,
Creating legends of winter's show.

With every laugh, the winter hums,
While silly snowballs bounce like drums.
It's a tapestry woven so bright,
Of funny dreams in frosty light.

## Echoes of a Crystal Heart

In the trees, the branches squeak,
With frosty laughter, all unique.
A handful of snow, a twinkling spark,
As snowmen wink in the chilly dark.

Icicles glisten, a chandelier,
But watch out! They might disappear.
As bunnies hop and stumble too,
They dream of pies, oh what a view!

Breezes whistle a silly tune,
While frosty friends dance 'neath the moon.
A snowball hits a cheeky face,
Watch them tumble, lost in space!

As winter whispers in the night,
The echoes laugh, oh what delight!
A crystal heart beats warm inside,
While playful spirits dance and glide.

## Shivers of Nostalgia

There's frosty air and frozen breath,
A snowman glares, oh what a test!
He's got a carrot nose, so fine,
But what's this? A squirrel's snack line!

The snow dips down, a comfy bed,
While little feet leave trails instead.
With snowflakes flopping in the breeze,
Each memory's wrapped like winter's tease.

A nostalgics' scream, "To the top!"
On icy hills, they spin and flop.
With snowdrifts hiding all their woes,
They'll cruise down fast, like winter's prose.

With every shiver, there's a tale,
Of winter's fun that will prevail.
Oh, what a season, fast and free,
With laughter echoing endlessly!

## **Icicles of Memory**

Stuck inside with hot cocoa,
Sipping dreams of frosty cheer.
I once saw a snowman dance,
He tripped and fell—oh dear!

Birds wear coats, what a sight!
Chickadees in stylish hues.
Watching snowflakes on their flight,
Wonder who makes the news?

Snowball fights and frozen toes,
I aim, I miss, it's such a blast.
My hat flies off in the throes,
And snowballs form much too fast!

Yet through all the winter's play,
There's laughter beneath the frost.
In memories like snow, they stay,
And warmth is never lost.

## **Love in a Winter's Grasp**

Wrapped up tight in woolen layers,
Two hearts giggle through the freeze.
We build a fort, become some players,
Oh, love, can bring you to your knees!

With every laugh, the snowflakes swirl,
A dance of joy on frozen ground.
Your nose is red, oh what a pearl,
I pull you close, there's love abound.

Mittens fight for the warmest space,
As we sip tea and share a grin.
Your snowy hat, quite out of place,
But matches perfectly with sin.

And though the cold is nipping near,
Our hearts keep beating soft and bright.
In winter's chill, I know you're here,
Together, we are pure delight.

## The Quiet Between Snowflakes

In silence, snow blankets the street,
And two friends share a laugh out loud.
We crunch along—so light on feet,
As snowdrifts form a feathery shroud.

We pause for a breath, the air so clear,
The world is hushed, a snowy dream.
But oh! What's that? A frozen beer?
Now that's a way to make us beam!

Snowman-building turns to a race,
Who can stack their carrots best?
When timing's off, it's all a chase,
And laughing hard, we forget the rest.

Yet in this stillness, friendship's glow,
Dances with the flakes that fall.
Each moment wrapped in winter's show,
Perfect, silly, and a bit small.

## **Frosted Echoes of Affection**

With cheeks as red as winter's fire,
You send a snowball flying past.
I duck in time, it's quite a sire,
Your laughter seems to echo fast.

We cozy up by the window's frost,
Hot chocolate spills, what a delight!
With every sip, we plan our cost,
Of snowball fights till late at night.

Frosted air, your breath like steam,
You wink at me, oh cheeky one!
We scheme again, a frozen dream,
Where laughter blooms like winter sun.

So here's to joys, both warm and bright,
In every flake, your smile's there.
Our hearts entwined in frosted light,
This love, a tale beyond compare.

## Enchantment in Each Snowfall

Snowflakes dance on frozen ground,
Where laughter echoes all around.
Snowmen tip their hats with glee,
As frosty breath sings joyfully.

Sleds race down the hills with flair,
With twinkling eyes and snow in hair.
A snowball flies with a playful throw,
Right at the friend who's moving slow.

Hot cocoa waits with marshmallow hugs,
While snowflakes settle like fuzzy rugs.
Winter's chill brings smiles so wide,
In a world where warmth can't hide.

With every flake, a giggly cheer,
The snow's sweet magic draws us near.
We twirl and spin in pure delight,
In the wonderland of winter's light.

## The Winter's Secret Whisper

Whispers of frost tickle my ear,
As snowflakes giggle, spreading cheer.
A cheeky squirrel in a furry coat,
Wonders who could ever float!

Icicles dangle like frozen jokes,
While snowmen tease with silly pokes.
Each snowball fight, a battle grand,
Where laughter rules, not a single plan.

Penguins slide and take a bow,
Here comes a rabbit, hopping how?
With winter's secrets swirling tight,
The world feels merry, pure delight.

Underneath the frosty trees,
A jolly scene that warms like tea.
In every flake, a tale unfolds,
Of whimsy, laughter, and hearts that hold.

## Solitude Wrapped in White

In solitude wrapped, I find my peace,
While snowflakes fall, all worries cease.
A quiet dance, the world drifts slow,
With each soft flake, new dreams do grow.

Alone with laughter, I twirl and spin,
The snow whispers secrets, let joy begin.
A penguin winks as it waddles by,
In this snowy realm, I reach for the sky.

Frosty landscapes, a peaceful sight,
While cheeky snowmen hold mock snowball fights.
The stillness broken by a playful shout,
In solitude shared, I never doubt.

With every breath, I taste the chill,
Yet warmth surrounds, my heart won't still.
Wrapped in white, I feel so spry,
In the joy of winter, I reach for the sky.

## **Heartfelt Resilience Under Ice**

Beneath the ice, a heart beats strong,
Weathering winter, where we belong.
A coat of frost, a brave facade,
Yet laughter blooms, it's never hard.

Slipping and sliding, we find our way,
With grace of penguins, come what may.
A snowball fight, oh what a scene,
Resilience wrapped in white so clean.

Frosty fingers hold fuzzy dreams,
While laughter flows in cheerful streams.
With mittens on, we twirl and laugh,
In this blustery dance, we find our path.

Heartfelt moments in cold's embrace,
We sing through the storms, finding our place.
Under ice, we still bring our cheer,
For laughter and love thrive through the year.

## Winter's Gentle Lullaby

Snowflakes dance on windows bright,
Chasing dreams in the pale moonlight.
Hot cocoa warms the one who sighs,
As chilly winds bring muffled cries.

Sledding down the hill is fun,
Till you land and lose your run.
With cheeks aglow, we laugh and play,
While snowmen sigh at our ballet.

In the chill, socks go missing fast,
As laughter echoes from the past.
The dog rolls 'round in snowy bliss,
While neighbors grumble—what's amiss?

Under layers, we stumble and trip,
Catching snowflakes with rosy lips.
Oh, winter's charms, they come and go,
But joy's our compass, through the snow.

## A Hearthbeat Amidst Ice

A crackling fire, a cozy scene,
With overcooked soup that's gone unseen.
I burn the toast, you laugh aloud,
While shadows dance beneath the cloud.

The snowman's belly, larger still,
Complains each hour that he can't chill.
With carrot nose and coal for eyes,
He teases us with frosty lies.

Inside, we wrap like burritos tight,
Warmed by love through the winter night.
Yet missed the mark—my wasabi stew,
Made you sneeze, but that's on you!

Outside we hear the world's delight,
While slippers squeak with every bite.
In our fortress of snow and cheer,
You'll find two hearts that persevere.

## **Flurries of Forgotten Love**

Oh, frozen fingers entwined in jest,
While frostbitten toes get little rest.
I slipped on ice, you found it grand,
   Challenging me to take a stand.

With snowflakes wiping every tear,
  We giggle at the year gone near.
But penguins cause the biggest fuss,
In love's sweet dance, we try not to cuss.

Sledding at dusk, oh what fun,
Till we land on our backs, both done.
I made you laugh until you cried,
While snowmen whispered, "Have you tried?"

In frozen puddles, we admire the stars,
While contemplating snowball wars.
With laughter echoing through the night,
  We cherish frost and love's delight.

## **Tucked Away in Tundra**

Bundled up, we brave the chills,
With laughter sparking, giving thrills.
A snowball fight becomes our game,
As icy missile drives you insane.

We build a fort that's strong and bold,
With secret snacks that never get old.
You found my stash of gingerbread,
And then you said, "It's time for bed!"

Frozen nose and chilly toes,
With shivers hiding all my woes.
And in this tundra, snug and sweet,
We find a winter skip in our beat.

So here we sit, as snowflakes fall,
With toasted marshmallows, we have a ball.
And though the frost might steal our breath,
It can't freeze this joyful zest.

## Love's Glacial Hold

In a blizzard of feelings, I'm lost,
Your laugh's like a snowflake, at no cost.
Chilled winds greet my heart each day,
Yet here I am, I wouldn't have it any other way.

Wrapped in layers, thick as a toast,
We trip on ice like a comedy ghost.
Your frigid touch and warm wit collide,
In a winter wonderland where our hearts abide.

The frost on your cheeks makes me cry,
Not from sadness, but a chilly goodbye.
Slip on the ice, it adds to the fun,
Our love's a snowball, let's dive and run!

So let the storm howl and snowflakes fly,
With you by my side, I float and sigh.
In this climate of giggles, then take your hand,
Let's make snowmen where the fun expands!

## **Shivering Beats and Winter Treats**

Your heart's a popsicle; it makes me shiver,
Like an ice cream cone that's starting to quiver.
Each laugh spreads warmth, even when it's cold,
I wrap my arms 'round, like a blanket that's bold.

Snowflakes fall and cover the ground,
With every slip, our giggles abound.
You say I'm frosty, but look at your nose,
In this winter dance, it's the warmth that glows!

Cocoa in hand, our fingers touch,
But oh! That ice, it's way too much.
With every breath, clouds of laughter rise,
The chill and thrill light up the skies.

So here's to winter, and all its charms,
Your icy heart, fits in my arms.
Let's sledge down hills and leave a track,
With fun in the snow, there's no looking back!

## **Icy Veils of Affection**

In your frosty gaze, I see a glint,
Like sunny rays when the clouds have a hint.
With every snicker, the winter air sparkles,
Breaking the ice, our love's little marvels.

Mittens paired, we stumble and slide,
Laughing so hard, we can barely decide.
You build a snowman, oh what a sight,
He looks like you—attire of white!

Our hands get cold, but my heart feels warm,
Amidst snowball fights, it's a delightful swarm.
Great winter tales, spun in the freeze,
With you, my dear, it's all fun and ease.

Under icy veils, our truth unfolds,
We dance 'round, ignoring what the world scolds.
In this winter chill, your laughter's the art,
Forever my treasure, that I call my heart!

## **Cold Nights, Warm Thoughts**

Nights are chilly; my socks are bizarre,
Yet here I sit, dreaming of our car.
Kisses that warm like summer's embrace,
Even when blizzards try to take their place.

Snow boots and snickers, it's quite a show,
Each icy stumble makes our laughter grow.
You're the fire in my frosty breath,
In this winter wonder, we cheat cold death.

Hot chocolate spills, oh, what a mess,
But you make the chaos feel like success.
Under flurries that tumble and prance,
Our hearts play a merry, yet clumsy dance.

Adventures on ice, with hearts that ignite,
In the cold of the night, your love feels so right.
So snug by the fire, let's keep it real—
In the snow's chilly grasp, with you, I can feel!

## **Frozen Paths of Longing**

In winter's grasp, I trip and fall,
With boots too big, I heed no call.
Snowflakes dance like playful sprites,
While I'm stuck in these frosty fights.

Icicles dangle, sharp and bright,
I swear they're plotting my next plight.
A snowball's tossed with aim so sly,
But all I've done is slip and cry.

With mittens thick, I wave hello,
To friends who laugh, they think it's show.
We build a man with carrot nose,
Yet I can't stand, and down I goes!

So here I lay, in snowy glee,
A frozen soldier, wild and free.
With every slip, a laugh I share,
In frozen paths, my heart's laid bare.

## Heartbeats in a Snowglobe

Shake me up, I spin around,
In this globe, sanity's drowned.
Snowflakes swirl, like thoughts in head,
As I juggle visions of toast and bread.

The cat's on skates, it's quite absurd,
Chasing its tail, away it stirred.
While I sip cocoa, spill on my shoe,
Oops! The best plans go askew.

The snowmen sneak their midnight dance,
With carrot hats, they take their chance.
While snowballs fly, I duck and weave,
In this wild game, can I believe?

So here I giggle, while covered in flakes,
I've lost the plot, but made some cakes.
With heartbeats fast, in joyous mess,
A snowglobe dream, nothing less.

## **Chasing Shadows in White**

With each step, I'm bound to slip,
Like trying to dance on a sinking ship.
The world is white, yet I see black,
Chasing shadows, but they won't track.

Snow boots squeak, a sound quite rare,
I skitter and slide, without a care.
A snow angel's made—but wait, who fell?
The ground is hard, a funny spell.

Laughter rings out, we build a fort,
But popsicle fingers aren't a support.
A snowball lands, my cheeks go red,
Oh, the laughter that fills my head!

Chasing shadows, both big and small,
In this winter wonderland, I have a ball.
As snowflakes twirl, I leap and run,
Here's to winter—oh, what fun!

## **Beneath the Bitter Chill**

Beneath the chill, my nose turns pink,
With thoughts of warmth, I start to think.
A cup of tea? No, hot cocoa's best,
But my marshmallows put me to the test.

Froggy hat pulled down so low,
I'm ready to face this freezing show.
But wait a sec, what's this I see?
The neighbor's dog just tripped on me!

Snowballs fly, though none are aimed,
Random misses, I'm so ashamed.
We slip and slide with radiant glee,
This frosty chaos is so carefree.

So beneath the chill, I find my cheer,
While juggling snowballs, I've conquered fear.
In every tumble, a giggle's found,
In wintry realms, joy does abound.

## **Frozen Wishes Unraveled**

Snowflakes fall, my nose turns red,
Hot cocoa wishes, I'd rather be fed.
Each sip a dream, but I spill with glee,
Drinking it fast, now it's all over me.

Snowmen stand tall, with scarves all askew,
They judge me too much; it's rude, don't you think?
I'd build one with style, a hat and a shoe,
But they just fall over; oh dear, what a stink!

Sledding downhill, I shoot like a dart,
Only to crash into my best friend's heart.
We roll in the snow; oh, what a delight,
Coughing with laughter, what a silly sight!

The night brings a chill, igloos fill with cheer,
We toast to frozen fumbles; oh dear!
Under a warm blanket, we giggle and chat,
Who knew snow could lead to such fun chit-chat?

## Heart Clocks Under Ice

Tick tock, it's cold, the clock's running slow,
I'm stuck in slow motion—what a tragic show!
Ice cubes in the drink, a comedy spree,
Laughter erupts like bubbles in tea.

A penguin waltz on slippery white,
Each step a dance, a comical sight.
The snow is my partner, oh how we glide,
Falling like leaves; there's no place to hide.

Icicles dangle like party hats worn,
They glimmer and shimmer; oh, how they adorn!
I twirl with a snowball, aiming for fun,
But it hits a snowman, now he's got a gun!

With each little thaw, the heart beats away,
Melting my worries, no cares left to fray.
We dance with the frost, wrapped in laughter's quilt,
In this frozen moment, my joys are all built.

## An Embrace of Sparkling Silence

In the quiet glow, the snowflakes all cling,
Not a peep, just giggles; oh, look, what they bring!
Like whispers of joy in a wintery dance,
Snow-globe moments, oh, give love a chance.

A snow angel flops, but she's missing her wing,
She's laughing it off; what a whimsical thing.
With each playful push, we tumble and roll,
The frosty chill wraps us, a giggly stroll.

Under winter's spell, with glitter and sighs,
We make snowman faces, oh my, what a surprise.
He winks at my crush; my heart takes a leap,
Caught in the frost, oh, love's just so deep!

As silence sparkles, we plot and we plan,
To throw snowball battles, oh, what a grand slam!
In the embrace of this shimmering cheer,
Our laughter is louder than any frontier.

## **Frosted Portraits of Love**

In a frosty museum, emotions displayed,
Our hearts captured forever, though ice may charade.
Each smile's a portrait, etched clear as a pie,
But watch out! A snowball's about to fly by!

The artwork of winter, a collaboration bold,
With snow-people striking a pose, oh so cold.
They tip their hats, as if to say,
"Join us for fun; don't waste this good day!"

Tickled by frost, I tread carefully here,
Unearthed by laughter, we'll conquer our fear.
With each frozen moment, our hearts start to race,
As love fills the canvas, oh, what a grand place!

So here we are, in this ice age of bliss,
Capturing joy in each frosty sweet kiss.
With portraits of laughter that twinkle with art,
This winter wonderland melts right to the heart.

## Reflections in a Crystal World

In a land where frost takes the lead,
Snowflakes dance like they're freed,
Puddles reflect our silly capers,
Falling down like unwelcome paper.

My nose is red, my toes are cold,
Laughing at snowmen, brave and bold,
They wobble, they tip, then they fall flat,
Saying cheese like a goofy cat.

We sled down hills, giggles galore,
The world's a giant, icy floor,
With every bump, we shout and cheer,
Winter's antics bring us near.

In this crystal world, we gleefully bounce,
Chasing each other, oh, what a flounce!
Frosty beards on friends so dear,
Catch a snowball - it's all in good cheer!

## **Hushed Conversations in Snowfall**

Whispers float on the chilly air,
Snowflakes gossip without a care,
A snowman thinks he's quite the charmer,
While snowflakes laugh, a warm up warmer.

Puppies bound, with tongues out wide,
Chasing each snowflake on their ride,
As if they're made of tasty treats,
While they trip on their own four feet.

Friends make angels with clumsy grace,
Landing hard, it's quite the face!
Winter's laughter echoes through,
As we slip and slide, oh, who knew?

Frosty cheeks and snowball fights,
Pranks played all through frosty nights,
With every scoop, a giggle shared,
In frost-kissed fun, we're fully snared!

## Canvas of Frosted Feelings

A canvas white, where thoughts take flight,
Painting dreams, with snow so bright,
Our laughter splashes, colors in the air,
While snowflakes wink, as if they care.

Frosted eyebrows, a sight to see,
As we wobble on sleds, just you and me,
With every tumble, we erupt in glee,
Like frostbitten trees, we're carefree!

Snowball evidence stains the ground,
Hidden goodies, nowhere to be found,
We waddle around like penguin fools,
In this frosted world, we break the rules.

Snowflakes melt, laughter will linger,
As we wave goodbye with cold, numb fingers,
Memories painted in icy blues,
On this canvas, we'll share our views!

## Winter's Tender Touch

Winter's touch is soft and light,
Wrapping us up in pure delight,
With every snowflake that falls from the sky,
We can't help but giggle and sigh.

Slipping on ice, oh what a sight,
Rolling in snow feels perfectly right,
A race to the warm, hot cocoa's the prize,
With whipped cream peaks that reach for the skies.

Our boots are heavy, yet hearts are light,
Building snow forts, preparing for a fight,
Snowballs fly like confetti in spring,
Laughter erupts with each silly fling.

As day turns to dusk, shadows grow long,
The chill of winter can't dampen our song,
In frosty gatherings, love's in the air,
With winter's tender touch, we'll always share!

## **Hearts Adrift in Flurries**

Snowflakes dance, they make us laugh,
Our hearts afloat, like goofy chaff.
With mittens stuck, we trip and slide,
In frosty chaos, we take each stride.

A snowman yawns, says 'Why so glum?'
He's got a carrot nose, that's quite the sum!
We sip hot cocoa, spill on our coats,
Laughter warms us, like comfy notes.

Snowball fights erupt, oh what a show!
With icy missiles, we duck and throw.
But love binds us tight, through chilly glee,
In flurries of joy, just you and me.

As night falls down, snow glows so bright,
We snuggle close, hearts feeling light.
Let winter whirl, let blizzards howl,
In frosty fun, we find our growl.

## **Resilience of Love's Frost**

Frosty morning, we brave the chill,
Tripping on ice with a tumble and thrill.
Giggles echo through the winter air,
Our hearts beat loud, without a care.

Snowflakes tease, like little sprites,
We stumble through, in snowy fights.
With scarves wrapped tight, and noses red,
We'll create a world where no one's led.

Slipping and sliding, oh what a sight,
Hot soup awaits by the firelight.
Through winter's grip, our spirits soar,
In every laugh, we find much more.

In snowball chaos, love's bright spark,
We dance through winter, leaving a mark.
With frosty kisses and wide-eyed smiles,
We'll conquer winter, through all its trials.

## **Bound by the Blizzard**

Caught in a blizzard, here we stay,
Snowed in together, come what may.
Socks mismatched, and cozy old shoes,
In our little world, we can't lose.

The wind howls loud, a comedic sound,
We laugh and dance, hearts unbound.
Cupcakes of snow, on each other's heads,
Love's in the air, in our snuggly beds.

Hot soup spills, a kitchen mess spree,
Laughter echoes, just you and me.
As the world outside turns to ice,
We've got each other, isn't that nice?

Chasing each other, through drifts so deep,
In goofy antics, our souls we keep.
Warmed by love, through winter's jest,
We'll laugh forever, and that's the best.

**Frozen Windows**

Through frosted panes, our breath appears,
Pantomime warmth, among winter's cheers.
We scribble hearts with snowy delight,
Giggling at shapes, in morning light.

Inside we cozy, outside it's cold,
Stories unravel, warm tales told.
We play with snow, a comical scene,
Like children again, so free and keen.

As snow drifts down, it paints us white,
We snuggle tighter, all through the night.
With cups of cheer and some silly jokes,
In our frozen world, love never chokes.

Beneath the blankets, with pillows galore,
We slide and glide, laughter in store.
In every giggle, a spark ignites,
Together through winter, our hearts take flights.

## **Open Hearts**

Snowflakes tumbling, a playful dive,
With hearts wide open, we come alive.
We giggle at squirrels, all fluffy and round,
In our comical world, joy is found.

Gusting winds push us here and there,
But in our laughter, we have no care.
With snowballs flying, the fun won't wane,
We embrace the flakes, like quirky rain.

Mittens mismatched, with one fallen flat,
It's love in the air, and there's plenty of that!
Through frozen moments, we'll cheer and prance,
Dancing through winter, in our own dance.

As dusk settles in, our spirits gleam,
In laughter and warmth, it's all a dream.
Together we find, in cold and in heat,
Open hearts melting, makes our lives sweet.

## A Serenade to Winter Love

In a frosty park, we dance, no grace,
You slipped and fell, left me in a trace.
We waltzed with snowflakes, what a sight!
Your hat flew off, a comical fright.

With hot cocoa, we toasted with cheer,
Missed your mouth, oh dear! Oh dear!
Your marshmallow nose is looking quite plump,
We giggled and drank, what a delightful clump.

Wrapped in blankets, we found our delight,
The power went out, no more Netflix tonight!
We played charades by candlelight glow,
You mimed a snowman—fell flat in the snow.

Yet love's a snowball, we toss with great care,
Laughter in winter, it's beyond compare.
So here's to our quirks, in this chilly embrace,
Winter's a riot, and we've got the grace!

## **Midnight Whispers on Frost**

The clock struck twelve, the world was white,
I slipped on ice, oh what a sight!
You laughed so hard, you nearly cried,
In the frosty air, our giggles collide.

Under the streetlamps, we made our path,
But surprise! A snowball launched—a silly wrath!
You ducked just in time, then started to plot,
We built a fortress, a snow-fighting lot.

With whispers of secrets, we hid in our fortress,
Sharing hot soup, just added more mess.
You spilled it on me, I gave you a look,
"Next time, less soup!"—that's how love cooks.

The moon watched us as we giggled and played,
In a world of frost, our laughter stayed.
So here's to the nights, where we frolic and roam,
In a snow-covered dream, we found our home!

## Longing Encased in Ice

In the winter's chill, I sent you a letter,
But a snowstorm struck, it got much wetter.
The postman slipped, my note in a flurry,
You read it out loud—was that a laugh or a hurry?

You wrote back in code, a puzzle to crack,
"Send chocolate!" you said, in a snow-suited whack.
I tripped on my way, what a dear little sight,
Cadbury wrappers flew, oh what a delight!

Encased in ice, our hearts began to skate,
I swirled too fast and ran into fate.
We crashed and laughed, tangled in romance,
In a world full of snow, we took a wild chance.

So let's bundle up, and make snow angels too,
Love in the frost, with wonders anew.
In winter's surprise, we'll find our warm glow,
In a whimsical dance, oh where else would we go?

## Glimmers of Hope Beneath Snow

Beneath the blanket, the world's a delight,
You made a snowman—quite the veggie sight!
With carrots for a nose, and sticks for the arms,
He winked at us both with his snowy charms.

While sledding down hills, with reckless delight,
You yelled "Look out!"—but I took off in flight!
Landed in bushes, how great was that fall?
You laughed till you cried, oh you quirky doll!

Our snow forts took shape, a battle ensued,
Snowballs as ammo, we both were quite rude.
But giggles erupted, as the snowflakes did fall,
Underneath all this fluff, love conquers all!

So toast with your cocoa, let's savor this cheer,
In this wonderland where joy is so near.
With laughter and warmth, we embrace every woe,
For there's hope that glimmers beneath all this snow!

Milton Keynes UK
Ingram Content Group UK Ltd.
UKHW020816141124
451205UK00012B/611

9 789916 945292